Tails
OF A
Lady
DOG CATCHER

Nancy LeBaron-Kiley

Fulton Books, Inc.
Meadville, PA

Published by Fulton Books 2022

ISBN 978-1-63985-944-3 (paperback)
ISBN 979-8-88505-176-7 (hardcover)
ISBN 978-1-63985-945-0 (digital)

Printed in the United States of America

All of my life I've been an animal lover, it's like a bug that bites you and the effects never wear off. No matter where I went, an animal would find me, sometimes needing my help, other times just to make me smile. Dogs especially had a connection with me. They would follow me home, most times with a lot of encouragement from me, but back then, there were no leash laws and I had a strong need to protect them from harm and harm came in many shapes; cars, other animals and bad people. I never really heard of or knew what a dog catcher was, but in the early 70's cartoons certainly did nothing for their image and it was an image that unfortunately was pretty much on target; a mean looking MAN with a net, a truck to lock them in and sad faced dogs. I had no idea that my animal connection background was going to throw me into this realm and that I would change the course of history not only for "dog catchers" but for women in the field of Animal Law Enforcement.

In the fall of 1972 I noticed a police cruiser at the end of my street and walked up to see what was happening, being nosey. Turns out the officer was trying to get a St. Bernard to obligingly put his head in a rope noose he was holding, quite funny actually, dogs aren't stupid. The St. Bernard was toying with him, made me giggle. The officer had the back door to the cruiser open also hoping the dog would hop in. Now most dogs do love a good ride, but you need to use the magic words, cookie and go for ride, obviously this patrolman was not a dog person and didn't talk dog. I stood there watching this and chuckling to myself when one of the neighbors yelled out "Show him how it's done Nancy!" So I walked over, took the dog by the collar, walked over to the cruiser and said "hop up", and he did. I shut the door and the neighbors started clapping, to the embarrassment of the patrolman. The officer took down my name and address for his police report and said in his report that I should be the dog officer. The local newspapers would scan police reports for news each day, no computers back then, and when they read the report it started the ball rolling. A lot of folks who knew me and that had read the article encouraged me to apply for a job that wasn't even available, but if you don't ask, you won't ever know. I made an appointment to see the Mayor. Mind you, I'm a 19 year old headstrong female who fears nothing with a what-the-hell attitude. What's the worst that can happen, they say no. The Mayor had read the report and evidently was impressed but I went to school with his daughter and I think she may have said something about my reputation with animals, just a hunch. Anyway, I met with him and he decided to hire me as a DPW laborer, assigned to the Dog Pound for a six week emergency period. The gentleman who was the Dog Officer at the time was in some hot water with the City Council for not answering complaint calls and basically being unavailable. On the first week as the Assistant Dog Catcher I rounded up 37 dogs and collected $93 in fines, something the City Treasurer had never seen before and reported not only to the Mayor but to the City Council and the newspapers. Me, I was having a great time riding around, catching dogs and for some reason getting a lot of attention from the press. The reporters followed me everywhere, taking pictures, asking questions and putting it all on the front page of the local newspaper. The City Council called in the Dog Officer who abruptly resigned. Now you don't really think they are going to give this position to a 19 year old FEMALE do you, of course not. Here I am doing a great job but I'm a girl. So, next in line is a police chauffer who knows absolutely nothing about dogs, REALLY?? Yep, he lasted three days and quit. Next up, an older gentleman, again, no dog experience and he is going to tell me what to do, I don't think so. I think he lasted a month. I had to break up a fight between two German Shepherds, which he was afraid of, and that got back to the Mayor. He thought it funny that I was the brave one for jumping into the fight while the Dog Officer looked on, but he also knew he had the hard decision to make. On June 9, 1973, less than a year after it all started, he officially appointed me the Dog Officer, the first female Dog Officer in the country, the first female Dog Officer in the City setting, the first female department head in the City of Peabody, Massachusetts and the youngest department head in the City and no one can break those records, I own them.

I had no idea what I was getting myself into. What did I know about budgets, bill schedules, City Council Meetings; I just wanted to continue having fun with all the animals. Of course I thought about a paying job with health insurance, but this was a dream come true. I also knew nothing about politics or politicians, and they had no idea who they were dealing with either, but those stories are for later. The Police Department was a group of great guys who looked on me as a little sister and most of them were willing to help me and protect me in their own little way. I can honestly say that I was *never* approached by any of them for a date but then again, I had access to things that they were afraid of and on occasion I did use them to my advantage. When I say this was the best job ever, I mean I had a lot of fun, not only with the animals but torturing the guys I worked with, I had sixty patrolmen scared to death of me, why you ask, because I had access to the things that they were most afraid of, snakes and rats! Keep reading, those stories will keep you laughing. It's funny; men can sound just like screaming little girls when scared!

Woman is appointed Peabody dog catcher

PEABODY — Nineteen year-old Nancy LeBaron broke the sex barrier Monday morning, when she was sworn in as dog officer, becoming the first female ever to hold that position in the city's history.

A whiz with animals, the young lady dog nabber has been a major contender for the top spot since she was appointed assistant dog catcher by Mayor Nicholas Mavroules last fall.

Since that time, three dog officers have come and gone, and Miss LeBaron had not captured the top job, even though many thought she deserved it.

It is believed she is the youngest city official ever to hold a major municipal post.

It was truly a day for women's lib, as Nancy LeBaron was sworn into office by Assistant City Clerk Natalie Maga.

June 8, 1973

The Dog Pound

When I got my first glimpse of the Dog Pound, to say it was heart breaking was an understatement. Picture a cinderblock building with a sink and four windows. The cages were chain link and stacked two high, so that any dog that peed or pooped in the top row eventually shared it with the dog below him. They were old, they were nasty and they were on my hit list. My first week there I went in and every day I found another dead dog. I had no clue what was happening and decided to call the vet that the City used. His name was Dr. Rivers and he asked me what I saw, as in nasal discharge etc. I gave him a blow by blow of everything I was seeing. He told me I had a bad case of distemper running through the pound. He told me that most likely all the dogs that were there were going to die from this, my world crashed in. This is not what I want to see and I'm sure the public would be outraged at how their dogs would be kept if caught by me. At the same time this is happening I get a visit from a few people with PETA, who the hell are they? People for the Ethical Treatment of Animals. They were not a welcome site, according to what I heard later, by most shelters. I have to say, they did right by me. They offered to come and help clean up the dog pound and showed up every day to help me bleach everything in the pound and helped me dismantle and toss out all the cages. I then went to the Mayor and lied. I told him the MSPCA had come in and condemned all the cages and that I had to dismantle and toss them out and now had no where to put dogs. I guess I was either lucky or had a good guardian angel looking out for the dogs because I received 13 various sized stainless steel cages, easy to clean and easy to keep dogs from contacting one another. It made a world of difference for the dogs. Now to work on getting fencing to put the dogs out during the day to get some fresh air, while I cleaned cages and got their meals ready.

The Dog Pound was also in the city dump. If you have never seen a dump rat, well, they are pretty big. I had a problem with them making a nest in my desk drawer. I would call the Board of Health and they would give me some wax sticks. All I was doing was feeding them. These things could eat and never seemed to go away. My frustration was building, not good to let me think about what to do next. I bought a Havaheart trap, those are the kind that catch animals without hurting them. I caught a great big rat and I found a nest of babies that had obviously eaten the poison because they were dead, in my desk drawer. I got some paper lunch bags, put a little dead body in each bag and picked up my trap with the live rat and headed to City Hall. My horns are out and I'm on a mission. First I went into the City Council chambers and put a little bag in each councilor's desk. That will be an interesting meeting. Then I went and got my live rat in the Havahart trap. I walked into the Mayor's office and set it down on his secretary's desk, slapped the side and that rat jumped up and down and made only a noise a rat could make, eeek, eeek, eeek. Now, Mrs. W. was a large woman, but she could run. I don't think her feet ever touched the floor! I yelled "Where is he?" While running down the hall she yelled back "Home". So, my new friend and I took a ride to the Mayor's house. He obviously had been warned I was coming. He opened the door and asked me what I wanted. I told him that if I had to work with rats so was everyone else and that I was going to trap and let them go in City Hall unless I got an exterminator. The exterminator was there the next day. I was a happy camper!

Down the street from the dump was a residential neighborhood and there was a young man, about 12 years old, who would come to the dump collecting bottles that he made things with. He liked animals and would often come in and help me. I felt I could trust Dan the man as I called him, and gave him a key to the dog pound. Winter was coming and I just had a feeling I was going to need a backup plan for the dogs. Smart move! We had a heavy snowfall and I couldn't get to the pound to feed or clean the dogs but Dan only had to walk up the road and he did. I paid him out of my own pocket to take care of the dogs on days I couldn't get there because of snow. Now I wasn't making a lot of money, I think my paycheck was $150 a week, but I'm not about to let the dogs go without food or water and sit in filth, so I tried to keep him happy with $5 a day. Dan never let me down. The pound also had no bathroom and when I asked for one to be installed, they shut the pound down and farmed it out to a vet in an adjacent town. That was actually a great thing for me because I didn't have to worry about the dogs during the bad weather and getting to the dump to take care of them. I did miss the guys I worked with at the dump and all the truckers that would come in and bring the dogs cookies. The City gave all the new cages they had bought to the vet with the promise that they would always have available space for my strays. Now the only thing wrong with this was that I could no longer ignore the 10 day law. The 10 day law meant that if a dog was not claimed or adopted within 10 days, they were to be euthanized. Don't worry, I found a way around that. I simply said I picked up another dog, filled out a new form and got another 10 days to find them a home. That was still no easy task and unfortunately some nice dogs didn't get the home they deserved or needed. The thing is; the adoption fee was $10.00 and a dog license. Today's world sees adoptions well over $500 and people have no problem paying that. How the world has changed. With people being very dog conscious these days and abiding by leash laws, you don't get the same variety of mutts that I had when there were packs of dogs running loose all over the place. Now you have your puppy mills cranking out designer mutts and people are actually paying big bucks for them. Oh, try to tell them it's a mutt and they get very defensive. If it's not a purebred, it's a mutt no matter what the combinations are. Buying them is contributing to puppy mills. Watch the ASPCA commercials, those are puppy mills folks, wake up. Check your rescues and verify they are legit by calling your State Department of Agriculture to see if they are registered in your state as a 501-3C, you may be surprised by how many are not. People abiding by the leash law has created a new genre, dogs from other countries being brought in for adoption, or from other parts of the U.S. I just think back at the poor dogs that I couldn't place and these changes bother me. I guess there is no good solution, packs of dogs running around or puppy mills or dogs from other areas up for "adoption". OK, I'm finished venting.

Skunks and Raccoons

Dog officer finds orphan

Nancy LeBaron was sworn in as Peabody Dog Officer by assistant City Clerk Natalie Maga Monday. She had been assistant dog officer and has become the fourth to hold the top position in the last year. Miss LeBaron has a unique way with animals and has proved worthy of her job. Here, she holds one of 4 baby skunks she found abandoned by the mother and has found homes for all of them.

I was officially the Dog Catcher, but in real life I handled any animal that needed my help. One of my first animal stories is of a raccoon that I thought had gotten away from a human home. He was in a back yard of a woman's home trying to turn on the water faucet for the hose when the owner of the home came upon him. He didn't seem wild in any way and they called me to come and get him. I watched him for a few minutes and decided he must have been tame, so I went and picked him up. He seemed fine. After a few minutes of patting him and checking him out he started to have a seizure and promptly bit down on my thumb, and died. Here I am, raccoon, dead, hanging onto my thumb. Now what? Okay, remove the coon from my thumb and take him to the Animal Hospital I use for injured animals. The vet comes out and looks at my thumb, takes a look at the coon and thinks, probably distemper based on the mucus in his eyes and nose, but let's test it to be sure. He tells his kennel keeper, not a bright bulb by any means, to take the raccoon into the barn and remove its head for rabies testing, which is what is done to any animal that is a suspected rabies carrier so the brain can be tested. Oh no, what does he do? He puts it in the crematory and cremates it. The vet is 99% sure it's distemper, so let's not worry about it. Nineteen year old naïve me, OK! Thinking back on that, what a dope I was. I'm here years later writing this, so I guess I didn't get rabies.

My reputation was out there now. I was getting calls for a lot of different animals and I was happy to take them and see what was in store on my next adventure, because all animal complaints were an adventure, at least for me.

I had numerous calls for skunks and they are the one animal no one wants to deal with but skunks are truly the gentleman or woman of the animal world. They are also the Magoo's of the animal world with the worst eye sight of any animal. Most of my calls were for skunks in window wells. You know, the windows that are below the ground with a curved well to keep them from flooding. That seemed to be a favorite place for a skunk to fall into, Mr. Magoo strikes again. Now if you don't know who Mr. Magoo is then you need to look that up on the internet, great cartoon. They also are not known for being good climbers. People would put a board into the window well thinking the skunk would climb out, not going to happen! So, I would get the call. I don't know where I got the knowledge or how I figured it out, but laying on my stomach, tapping the ground, waiting for the skunk to lift its tail and then making a quick grab for the tail worked. As long as their feet were off the ground, they couldn't spray. I just lifted them out and gave them a little toss away from me and off they went on their merry way. No spray, no problem. They also will warn you in a way only a skunk will. If you approach them and they see you, they will run, but if cornered they will run towards you and stomp their feet. Take the hint, get away or you're going to smell pretty bad. Skunk spray is an acid, so no, your tomato juice won't work because it is also an acid. You need baking soda and any guy worthy of doing mechanical work on your car knows that when you put baking soda on battery acid, it dissolves. Same thing happens with skunk spray. If your dog gets hit, always in the face, take some baking soda and mix it with milk and pour it into the side pocket of your dog's mouth. The baking soda will neutralize the spray and the milk will curdle causing the dog to throw it all up and make him feel better. Then you mix a batch of baking soda and water to a paste consistency and rub it all over your dog's face and let it dry. This neutralizes the acid and when you brush it off the smell is gone. Believe me, this is the only thing that actually works, used it many times.

One of my favorite stories about skunks starts with a hotel called the Colonial Hilton. They called me one night telling me they had a skunk in the elevator shaft. Now this was in another town and I was on my own time, but my reputation had made it to the manager's ear. They called me. First thing they asked, "Can you guarantee it won't spray"? NO!

"Ok, can you help us anyway"? Sure. I went to the hotel and just down the hall from the main dining room, (I saw all this on the way in and thought well this is going to be a quick evacuation as I chuckled to myself), was the elevator shaft that housed my prey. I found the young skunk, tail down, good sign, you never want to play with a skunk who's tail is up because that means someone has aggravated him enough that he is locked and loaded and ready to spray. I did my usual laying on my stomach, tapped the floor and up came the tail; I made a quick grab and got him. Now the fun part! I walked out of this hotel holding a skunk by the tail, past the dining room, shocked a lot of people and out the door we went. There in front of me was a stretch limo, driver leaning on the passenger side waiting for his clients to come out and having a smoke. Oh joy, more fun. He saw me, saw the skunk and that's when I said "We're ready". He said a four letter word beginning with F, jumped into the driver's side and sped off: I obviously ruined someone's ride home but had myself a good giggle. I walked over to some bushes and gave the little guy an easy toss and off he went.

Not all of my skunk stories involved a real skunk. One of the guys on the force had a friend with a business of selling kids toys at fairs. He told me how he had a bunch of real looking animal puppets he thought I would like, so I stopped over to check it out. Well, he had a great skunk puppet. Perfect size, perfect color and when you put your hand in and rested his little face in the crook of your arm and wiggled your fingers, it looked dam real. Oh my evil brain lit up like a Christmas tree. Who can I try this out on? I started driving around and there came my opportunity, a road job. There was my friend Larry directing traffic. Now Larry was old enough to be my father but he had a good sense of humor. I pulled up, put my hand in the skunk puppet and hollered over for Larry to come see my new pet. Larry was also a big animal fan. He came over, saw the puppet and backed off, normal reaction. I told him not to worry that he was very friendly and wouldn't spray and that he could pat him. What a dope Larry was! He slowly reaches in to pat my pet skunk and when he got just close enough I quickly made a motion towards him with the skunk and made a PFFFFFT noise. Larry jumped back, his police hat flew into the street and got run over, I am in tears laughing while he is beating the snot out of me through the window and calling me all sorts of names. Sorry, still laughing. He then started laughing, still calling me names but amused by the whole situation. It took a good ten minutes for us both to stop laughing. OK, onto my next victim. Driving around, trying to think who can I get next? All of a sudden, out of the air crackles the radio and its Jonesy, the desk officer, brain lights up again. I walk into the station, skunk on my hand and resting in the crook of my arm, very realistic, cleared out the vestibule of visitors. Jonesy had his back to the whole scene and I'm thinking this gets better all the time. I did the same thing to Jonesy as I did to Larry, only problem was that his chair had wheels. He jumped, chair left the scene and Jonesy was on the floor. Me? Laughing!!! Seems Jonesy had a three day injury vacation because of me and my puppet. Got called into the Chief's office. *Oh oh.* "Bring your skunk puppet with you!" *Oh oh.* Chief says, "Give me that dam puppet". I said "What are you going to do with my skunk puppet?" He opens his desk drawer and pulls out the UZI. *Oh oh.* "You can go now and don't let me see anymore puppets in my station!" I never did see my puppet again, but heard he made for good target practice. I really liked him and had fun with him; guess I had a little too much fun.

Pay back for my skunk puppet wasn't a long ways away though. I had to pick up an injured skunk and of course, a smelly injured skunk. No vet in the area wants to deal with an injured skunk, for obvious reasons, so I had to take him to a wooded area and have a patrolman come and dispatch him, BUT…I had a new perfume on. I really don't mind the smell of skunk, but I'm pretty much alone in that department. I walked into the control room on the pretense of asking a question and who just happened to be there, the Chief. Oh joy, revenge of the skunk puppet. Before I could say anything my aroma arrived first. Chief says "OHHHH, you stink!" I threw my arms out and yelled "HUG" and ran towards him. Thankfully he wasn't carrying that day or he probably would have sent off a round in my direction. Boy could that man run! I got sent home, with pay. Can't tell you how many times I would pick up a dead skunk just to get a day off, worked every time.

The guys in the station weren't my only targets. I had a raccoon call to go to and was heading down one of the main streets in Peabody. We had had a lot of rain and the streets were narrowed by all the puddles. One poor fireman's house was right on the road where a huge puddle had collected and even though there was a drainage trap, it was clogged. He was out there in his big old fireman boots, you know, those tall ones that you can't move too fast in and he was trying to clear the trap. I came around the corner and saw him. Oh oh, brain just lit up again but this time the brain didn't react, the foot did. I floored it! He turned around and saw me coming and he said he knew what was going to happen the minute he saw my face. I hit that puddle at 45 mph and a tsunami hit him! OMG, I had to pull over down the road, I was laughing so hard. As I sped away all I saw was his fist in the air, cracked me right up. I'm in trouble again! He didn't report me, he just managed to take away the ladder I used to get up a tree to try to get an injured raccoon out of. It ain't no fun being stuck in a tree with a very angry raccoon with no way to get down. Eat crow, had to apologize before the ladder would come back. Okay, I can dish it out and take it, but I would laugh anytime I saw him and he would ask everyone around us, "Do you know what she did to me?" Still laughing my friend, RIP.

Judge Tiffany and Angel

I found the best teacher in the world when I met Judge Tiffany. First he was an animal lover, but an avid bird watcher first and foremost. He knew I was trying to do right by the animals and he also knew that the DA's of those days felt it beneath them to take on animal complaints. He called me into his chambers and told me that he was going to teach me the animal laws and that he expected me to cross all my T's and dot all my I's to close the loopholes on my complaints.

He took down Mass Law book, chapter 140 and we went to the licensing laws and then we moved onto the cruelty law, which he was very adamant that I know how to investigate, how to construct my complaint and how to Shepardize the law. Now Shepardize is when the law has an amendment added or deleted to it before a new version is printed, they send out that amended law and it is attached to the front of the chapter it belongs to. You have to know to look up your law first in the amendment section, if you find no amendment, then you go to the law you want and go from there. Read it, learn it, memorize it and use it as it is meant to be used. Most of my cruelty cases were before him more for teaching someone that the way they did things in the old country they came from, where not acceptable in America. No, you can't keep your six dogs squished into a rabbit hutch. No, you can't keep a ferret for a pet, back then they were illegal to own. No you can't own more than three dogs without a kennel license. Yes, your six pound house dog, now known as a pocketbook dog, needs to be licensed, it is still a canine, doesn't matter if it never leaves your pocketbook, oh the stupidity I endured!

The judge and I had many conversations and debates on laws, I think he enjoyed it as much as I did, but the knowledge that he gave me was the best thing that could happen to the animals that I was charged with protecting. I didn't lose my cases; I presented cases that even the DA had to pat me on the back for, thanks to the judge.

Angel

Not all of my calls were fun or funny, there were some heartbreakers too and Angel was one of them.

I got a call that someone heard a dog barking behind one of the local bars that had a vacant lot behind it with some small buildings and a dog pen. I took a ride down and located what appeared to be an abandoned dog pen. There was a dog house, but the lock on the gate was rusted and there were no dishes or even any dog poop. I also saw no dog but maybe there is one in the dog house, NO, there would be bowls for water and food, and dog poop, but I called out anyways. There was a faint bark coming from the dog house. It sounded like a small dog, I kept calling to it. Out from the darkness of the dog house came a large head, but I heard a small voice barking. Maybe there are two in there. Nope. She dragged herself out of the doghouse and over to me standing next to the fence of the dog pen. OMG, a shepherd, a paralyzed shepherd, a skin and bones paralyzed shepherd, my jaw dropped. The ground in the pen was a small stone base, certainly something you would not want to walk across barefoot and the tops of her back feet were raw and bleeding from being dragged over it. SHIT, I have no food with me was my first reaction. Seeing something so skinny you just want to feed it to make it feel better. Calm down, think!!! I immediately got on the radio, called for a sergeant, called for the police photographer and for the fire department with cutters to snap the lock. First on the scene was the sergeant and he was horrified at what he saw. He called to see when the photographer would be there and we discussed how to proceed. The Fire Department arrived next. To say the guys were sick at what they saw was an understatement, they were also mad to see that someone had left this poor dog in this condition. They wanted to break the lock so I could get the dog to the vet, but we had to wait, I needed the photographer to get pictures of the rusted lock, the lack of bowls of water or food or poop. It wasn't long before the photographer arrived and started snapping pictures of the lock, the pen, the dog, the sores on her feet, we took pictures of everything. I went to lift the dog into my truck and my mind is in German Shepherd mode and my brain is at the 65 lb average thin shepherd point, but she is not anywhere near that. When I got her to the vet and we weighed her, she was 27 lbs. We assumed that there was no poop in her pen because that was all she had to live on, disgusting I know, but there was no other conclusion to be drawn. Someone was watching over her that day because she had on a collar with a license! GOTCHA!!!

I left her at the vet's and went back to the station to look up her license. She belonged to a guy who lived across and down the street from the bar. Her license showed her name was Angel. I sat and wrote out my court complaint, I read it several times and had the sergeant read it as well before I went to the court to file cruelty charges against the owner. I'm not going to call him and tell him I have his dog, let's see if he even knows she's missing. It takes several days for the complaint to be processed, the warrant to be issued and the police to deliver it, no call from this jerk about his dog. The newspapers got hold of the story from reading the court papers and ran it on the front page with the guys name and address. Seems he was a martial arts instructor, maybe that's how the poor dog was paralyzed, a good kick to the back, who knows, she couldn't tell me, but I'm going with that. The papers asked about her status and because she was now considered evidence, she needed to be kept at the hospital and needed a water type bed to lie on because of the sores and her skinny condition. I read in the paper about two young boys standing out on the median in front of the local shopping mall collecting money to buy Angel a water bed and they collected enough to get her one, there are good people in the world thankfully. The dirt bag owner found himself on the receiving end of some threats. Someone actually walked up to his four year old son and told him to take a note into his dad. The note read that they were going to do to him what he had done to his dog. The family had to move but he still had the court case pending against him. He obviously had dealings with the court system before and knew how to play it. First you change venues, so the case moved to the Salem Court. Then you start asking for continuances for all kinds of reasons hoping the complainant, me, won't show up and you can get a dismissal. This dirt bag found out the hard way that when this pit bull latches on to you for cruelty, I don't let go. I was standing in the hallway of the court for one of these continuances when I noticed a sign on one of the offices that said "If you are the victim of a crime, you are entitled to be in the Victim/Witness Program in the state of Mass. I walked in and told them I wanted Angel in the program. The lady said, "It's a dog". I said "Where does it say on your sign that it has to be a person?" She is a living being and has been the victim of a crime. Angel became the first animal in the Victim/Witness Program in the State of Massachusetts. What does that mean? I get more money out of the dirt bag and hurt him in the pocket, basically. I was at every continuance until one day, he and his lawyer didn't see me standing at the back of the courtroom. His lawyer told the judge that he had been feeding the dog and showed an empty bag of dog food. Must have got that from a friend to try and show he fed the dog, mind you, it was now almost two months after I seized her. Before I could even say anything, the judge had obviously seen me back there an said "Officer, did he feed the dog?" I said "Would you like to see the pictures I have your honor?" Judge's reply, "Nope. Guilty!" "You are not allowed under the law to own a dog for two years, you owe $3500 for the veterinary hospital care and another $1200 for the Victim/Witness Program fee, which also helped pay for the hospital cost, plus a $1000 fine. After the case was over the local police were riding by my house and shining a light in my windows. I called the station to find out why and was told that the dirt bag was threatening to kill me. Really??? I have a gun, not worried.

Angel, unfortunately, was no longer evidence and tried as we did, no one wanted to take a dog on that first was paralyzed and second, when an animal is starved to that point, keeping food, even in small amounts, from shooting out the other end is a long process and her age made that difficult as well. Angel was humanely euthanized.

Judge Tiffany had taught me well and I will forever be grateful for all the animals I was able to get justice for because of him.

Snakes Are So Much Fun

When dealing with animals you learn that people exaggerate. I never believed the call fully, I had to see what the complainant was talking about in real time. So I took a call from a woman who told me that she lived on a curve, not a corner and she had a bush on that curve and when the kids were walking around the curve by the bush a big black snake would come out and chase them. Right! Have to see this one to believe it. I went to her street and parked across from the curve. As luck would have, here come two elementary kids walking to school. As they started past the bush, sure enough, out came a very large, fat black snake. Brain lights up! I have to catch this, just to see what kind of snake it is. I jump out of my truck and the chase is on.

It slithers into the bushes by her house and I'm in there trying to catch it, she is standing on her porch screaming that I'm going to get killed. "Lady, it's a snake, it's not poisonous (I hope)." I grabbed him, had him right behind his jaws like a good snake catcher would do, I'm so proud of myself. He proceeds to wrap his body all around my arm, but not squeezing, just holding on. With him on my left arm, I radio in that I need a log number (needed to make out a report) on a big black snake I just caught. *SILENCE*, nothing on the radio. Brain lights up again. This could be fun. I drive back to the station and park in the front so I can go into the vestibule and then into the control room and show off my snake to the boys, heehee. The vestibule in the station had bulletproof glass with a hole big enough to get your arm through and to talk to people through. A gun fit nicely too. The Chief was standing there and he had his gun out the hole in the glass and pointed at me. "Get out of my station NOW or I'll shoot you, you SOB." "But Chief." "NO, GET OUT!"

What I had wanted to do, after scarring everyone with it of course, was to call a doctor that works in the ER at the hospital up the road who just so happened to be a herpetologist and find out what kind of snake this was. Well, I just got kicked out of the station, so I took a ride to the ER with the snake still wrapped around my arm. No cell phones in those days. I walked in and went to the nurse's station and asked if Dr. O was in. One of the nurses said she would go get him for me. I'm checking out my snake, not paying any attention to anything when the doctor came out of the ER. His eyes lit up when he saw the snake. He told me it was a black pilot snake, a very nice specimen and then told me that the next time I have a snake to please wait outside for him. Seems I had cleared out the ER of all waiting patients and the nurses' station was now totally empty. I took the snake and released it behind the station in the woods, plenty of food, water and no one to bother him. I couldn't even get the photographer to grab a picture of him for my records. I also found all the doors locked when I got back to the station, they wouldn't let me in.

Being the only female in the Police Dept also got me the job of babysitter for female prisoners or picking up females on warrants. This one particular day I had to go with a patrolman over to Salem Court to pick up a female on a warrant and bring her back to Peabody Court. On the way out of the Peabody Court I saw one of the State Troopers I was friendly with. I have no idea why I said what I said, but it came back to get me. As I passed by him I said "Reggie, have I got something for you!" We got into the cruiser and went to Salem Court to bring back the female prisoner. We had just arrived there when over the loud speaker of the Court my name is being called to come to the Clerk's Office. The prisoner is in the holding cell, not the Clerk's Office. Why am I being summoned to the Clerk's office? I get there and she asks me "What did I do to Reggie?" I started laughing. If I'm getting blamed, it must be something good! I told her I didn't do anything. She told me I had better get back to Peabody Court because he was going to kill me. *Oh oh*, I'm in trouble and I didn't do anything.

We got back to the Peabody Court and here was Trooper Reggie, running around his car, calling me all sorts of names and asking me how I got into his cruiser. I look over and here is Trooper Dunphy, scowly expression on his face. When the troopers are in the Academy for training they are taught how to make a scowly expressionless face. You turn your lower lip up towards the top lip and lower your eye lids to look mean. I walked up and stood next to him. I asked him "What did you do?" "Don't know what you're talking about maam." I said, "Dunphy, he is going to shoot me!" "Don't know what you're talking about, maam." Seems Dunphy had found a garden snake in the bushes and knowing Reggie is a snake phobe, popped the lock on Reggie's cruiser and put the snake in the glove compartment. Reggie got in and was heading down the street when the snake escaped out the back of the glove compartment, dropped down to the floor and slithered under the front seat. He pulled a whole shot in the middle of the street and shot back into the Court House parking lot. He was still screaming obscenities at me as I left and to this day, he believes I did it. I told him it was something I would do, but that I really couldn't take credit for it. He still doesn't believe me.

Mechanic confronts snake-in-the-dash

By BRION O'CONNOR
News Staff

DANVERS — Brian Pelletier's retirement may come a little sooner than expected after the Ocean Pontiac mechanic found a three-and-a-half-foot boa constrictor in the dashboard of a customer's car.

"The owner brought the car in —a brand-new car —complaining the air conditioner wasn't working," said Pelletier, a mechanic 25 years. "I was laying right there on the floor, unscrewed the dash, and all of a sudden I looked over and six inches from my head there was this snake.

"I was going to retire in three years, but I think this will move it up," he said, and that he was considering charging the owner about $10 to get my heart started again."

Despite a curious crowd of almost two dozen mechanics, salespeople and Danvers police

SNAKE

(Continued on page 8)

William Ramsey of the state's Environmental Police and Nancy Kiley of Danvers, former Peabody animal control officer, free a boa constrictor from the console of a car at Ocean Pontiac Wednesday. *The Salem News/David Mutt*

This next snake story supposedly made it into the National Enquirer. In August of 1988 I got a call from my friend Bill, an Environmental Police Officer, previously known as Fish and Game, about a snake in a car and he asked for my help. Bill didn't like to handle reptiles of any sort. He told me that a gentleman had driven his car back from Ohio and couldn't get the air conditioner to work. At the dealership they removed the top of the console between the bucket seats and found a snake curled up around the wiring. Bill had no idea what kind of snake it was at the time, but he wasn't touching it. I told him I would help and arranged to meet him.

You have to picture a parking lot filled with car dealers, mechanics, the people waiting for their cars to be serviced and Fish and Game, along with a couple of cruisers, nosey people. I pulled up in my four door F350 dually pickup truck and jumped out. One female and a lot of scared men, what a scene. They all wanted to know what I was going to do. I don't know what I'm going to do until I see what the situation is. We made our way over to the car with all the doors open and no one near it. I went to the passenger side of the vehicle to have more space to work away from the steering wheel and had the mechanic looking in on the driver's side. The car then became surrounded by the nosey men and a photographer that I never saw in all of this commotion. I looked in and a light yellow snake was all curled up and wrapped around some wires. I couldn't see his head, but if you want to see a sleeping snake's head, just tap his body. I gave him a tap and up popped the dragon! I made a fast grab and had him behind his jaws. Good snake grab! I looked around to see where Bill was, I was now all by myself. The crowd had all disappeared to about 20 feet away which shows I'm in the midst of a pack of snake phobes. I started to slowly lift the snake helping him uncurl himself from the wires and found Bill looking in beside me and the photographer taking our picture. Bill was photo bombing! We had a pickle bucket with a lid we put the snake in and called a local animal petting zoo. Bill took charge of the snake in the bucket, after making triple sure the lid was on tight and took it to the petting zoo. The owner of the petting zoo checked out the snake, a Ball Python at about 2 ½ feet in length. He had room and would be happy to take it. We never found out how the snake got there but it made for a good story. Bill and I both heard that the story made the National Enquirer when UPI picked it up out of the local paper.

Another exaggeration that actually wasn't was the lady with hedges full of snakes. Snakes shed their skins and the best way for them to get the old skin off is to crawl through hedges or deep dry grasses. Seems this lady had finally badgered her son into trimming the hedges for her. He went out with his trimmers and found a lot of snakes crawling through them. He threw down the trimmers and ran into the house screaming, he wasn't ever trimming those hedges. She gave me a call and explained how it took her a long time to get her son to trim the hedges only to find snakes and now she would never get them done. Snake phobe. Yada, yada, yada. I took the ride up to see for myself and radioed in that I needed a log number for a snake call. Silence over the air, I had to laugh, I know what they are all thinking. We had some heavy winds the night before and a lot of branches were down in yards and this woman's yard was loaded with dead branches and leaves. I walked around the yard where the hedges were and sure enough, lots of snakes, mostly garden snakes but a couple of nasty ones in there, a black racer and a hog nose. She asked me to please get rid of as many as I could as she tried to convince her son to trim the hedges when I was done. I asked her if she had a deep box I could have to put them in and she did. I started collecting snakes. As I was collecting snakes one of the area patrolmen showed up to watch, from a distance. I had a bunch in the box when I saw a black racer in an arborvitae bush. I hollered over to Richie, the patrolman, and asked him to find me a long branch while I kept my eye on the snake I wanted to get. I'm patiently waiting, watching the snake and wondering what he is doing. I took my eyes off the snake and turned to look at Richie. He is walking with a long branch in his hands when all of a sudden he steps on a small branch that pops up and hits him in the leg. He threw down the branch he was carrying, started screaming like a little girl hollering he had been bitten by a snake, I am in tears laughing. Had I not seen it, I wouldn't have believed it. He runs to his cruiser and jumps in. I hollered over that it was a branch but he just threw a few choice words my way and sped off. I lost the black racer, couldn't find him. The woman was watching me out her front door and as I grabbed a snake she asked me if I was afraid of being bitten. I told her that garden snakes didn't have teeth, not to worry. Just then, the one I was holding bit me. Seems garden snakes have one tooth, called a milk tooth. Once they lose it, it doesn't grow back. So here I am, woman watching this happen, sees the tooth sticking out of my finger. I just looked at her and said "I lie." I ended up with a box of snakes, oh joy, torture time. Police station here I come. They didn't think to lock me out this time. Now I had to let the hog nose go, but not until I had a picture of him. He would sit up and strike out at you like a cobra, nasty temperament! Can't have fun with you! It's almost lunch time! I wonder who has brought in their lunch and stored it away in the fridge. I think I will serve up a little snake for lunch, hee hee. I took the biggest garden snake and put him in the fridge. Don't worry, he wouldn't be in there long enough to be affected by the cold. I have to find a place to hide quickly and watch, I hear footsteps coming down the steps to the lunch area. Two of the guys are yakking and head in and open the fridge. The screaming starts. OMG, I'm on the floor laughing. Oh oh, the Captain is one of my victims. I'm in trouble again. You really can't be mad at someone laughing as hard as I was because every time he opened his mouth to yell at me I laughed harder. He gave up. I was told that the next time I tried bringing a snake into the station I would be permanently locked out. Well, it wasn't long after that the call came into the control room, not to my phone line, that some-one had found a 15 ft Boa. I happened to be out on the road when that call came over the radio and after they gave me the information about the snake-SILENCE. This should be interesting. As it turns out, someone had thrown their dead boa in a dumpster. This was a very large, fat snake, very well taken care of before it died but I had no way of knowing who it may have belonged to. I didn't even know we had a snake that large in the City, if it in fact came from someone living in Peabody. Now, you really don't think I am going to tell them that the snake is dead. I just asked for my log number for a 15 ft boa. SILENCE again. I went back to the station to make out my report. Doors locked. *Really guys?* I told them the snake was not alive and that I left its body where it was found in the dumpster. They didn't believe me and sent someone out to make sure. They made me move about 10 feet away from my work van, and then looked in the win-dows to make sure I had no snake in there. Not a trusting lot, not that I blame them. I was allowed in but the Captain's door was open for him to have full view of my actions. Chicken!!!

Of course this is the same man who is also scared to death of mice. I was sitting at my desk doing some work and heard this bang, bang, bang, not a gun, something hitting the floor. The Captain's door was shut and all of a sudden I heard "Nancy, get in here quick." I opened his door and he yelled "Shut the door, hurry up". He was holding his police baton in his hand. I asked him what he was doing. He turned to look at me and in this straight face said "Mouse". I burst out laughing. He says "It's not funny!" Maybe not to him but it was a hoot to me. I told him to go get a cup of coffee and to shut the door on his way out, more to make him feel better than to keep the mouse in. The door had a half inch clearance, easy exit for the mouse. I saw the mouse in the corner, obviously traumatized by the beating it almost had and grabbed it. Poor thing was shaking. I took him out the back door and let him go. The Captain avoided going back in his office the rest of the day.

Now anyone with a mouse fear is easy prey for someone like me. Take for instance the time we had a prisoner who had a white mouse in his pocket, it was his pet. The desk man didn't search this man's pocket when he was brought in so they didn't know it was in there and when the prisoner laid down to take a nap in the lockup, they saw on the video camera a little white mouse come out of his pocket and walk around. I was called in to get the mouse. This is his pet, not bothering anyone so I'm trying to figure out a way out of this. Ahh, the Captain is a mouse phobe. I saw him leave the control room and saw my opportunity. I went into the ladies room and took a handful of toilet paper and fashioned a toilet paper mouse with a tail. Oh oh, I'm going to get in trouble again, but I'm laughing already inside thinking about the screaming I'm about to hear. I walked into the control room and the Captain immediately asked if I got the mouse. I said yes and threw the toilet paper mouse at him. Ok, someone pick me up off the floor, I am in tears laughing and he is heading for the door. I earned a lot of nasty names while working with the guys.

It wasn't just the snakes or mice though. I once put a shark's head in the men's room toilet, not a big shark, but big enough to scare the crap out of you! I stood outside the door to the men's room and sang the theme from Jaws, dondo dondon don. The screaming could be heard all over the station. LAUGHING! The guys didn't think it too funny. I would also wait for one victim, poor Jonesy my favorite victim, to walk down the hall towards the bathroom with the newspaper under his arm. I know what you are going to do! I would wait. After about two minutes I would kick open the door and yell "Jonesy, whatcha doin?" Oh, he hated me in the morning. He finally decided, after many episodes to maybe take care of business before he came to work. Took all the fun out of my day!

Exotics

Kinkajou

It's hard to believe that a Dog Officer would have the opportunity to handle exotics, but I did. My first experience was with a kinkajou. It happened on a cool fall night, it was dark but the banks were still open. I got a call from one of the banks located on a busy route that ran in front of the largest mall in the area. They claimed to have a monkey in the bank. I'm thinking, exaggeration but I'm excited, what animal could this call be about to elicit this description. I walked in and saw this animal; I have no idea what it is, lying on the teller's window counter eating an apple. Everyone wanted to know what it was, including me. I have no idea and have never seen one. It seemed friendly enough. I picked it up and put it in a crate to take back to the station. At the station I took it out for all the guys to see. The City was unprotected that night for a short time, all of the patrolmen came in to see this creature. The local newspaper had arrived too and was taking pictures. We didn't have internet at that time or cell phones, no way to look this up. The kinkajou had found one of the deskmen's lunch bag with his supper in it, that also had a pear inside. He wanted the fruit, so obviously, I have a fruit eater, but I still have no clue what it is. About three hours later the desk man got a call from the kinkajou's owner. Seems he was a traveling salesman and kept the kinkajou with him for company. He had picked it up in Panama along with a sloth. He also wanted to sell the kinkajou and it found it's forever home to a couple who lived in Peabody.

Now any animal persons dream, well at least mine was, is to catch a big cat, I'm talking Mountain Lion, Tiger, BIG CAT. Never going to happen in a city in Massachusetts you think. You're wrong. I received the call from dispatch, two lion cubs on Rte. 1 at the jug handle. The jug handle is a turn around on the highway used to change directions. Two lion cubs and a dog were out on the side of the highway roaming around. Evidently, as the story goes, a man from Canada had rescued a mother lion, which was pregnant and a monkey from someplace in Canada and was traveling the East Coast raising money and awareness of their plight. He owned an old school bus he had rigged up with cages for the monkey, the lion and two cubs she gave birth to and he had his dog to keep them all company. He decided to stop for a cup of coffee. He had the monkey tied but out of his cage while he drove the bus along with the cubs who he had tied together to keep them from jumping around the bus while he drove. The cubs loved the dog and followed the dog everywhere. The man found a spot to park his bus, got out and closed the door. Ever hear the phrase "monkey see, monkey do"? The monkey watches how the door is opened by the handle and had the time to get it open while the gentleman was in getting his coffee. The dog sees the open door and decides to go out and the cubs follow. The site of these animals caused quite a scene on the highway, people stopping, not knowing how to help, but taking plenty of pictures. The phones started ringing off the hook not only to the Police Station but to the State Police Barracks on the same stretch of road. A trooper got there before me and had the cubs and dog in his cruiser, so we decided to head for the barracks and wait for someone to call. Wasn't a long wait. The gentleman came in with all the paperwork from the Department of Agriculture allowing him to have them, I was hoping he didn't have any paperwork so I could take them home, they were so cute. They weren't the little guys you might be picturing. They were the size of a medium dog, about four months old. When I saw them again six weeks later at the local mall, they had grown to the same size as their mum. I couldn't believe they had grown that much in such a short span of time. I still enjoy looking at the pictures of them and the dog. I also have the newspaper article with a picture of the Capuchin monkey sitting in the bus, the troublemaker.

George of the Jungle looks out the window of the school bus in which he travels. It was George who freed his animal companions on Rte. 1 yesterday morning.

Trooper Barry Jordan tries to make friends with one of two lion cubs which escaped on Rte. 1 yesterday, after George of the Jungle freed them from their cages. (Times photos by Bruce Bowman)

Revenge, Nope

So sooner or later the guys are going to have revenge on me for all the rotten things I did. They found their opportunity, they thought, in the Hell's Angels motorcycle club. The president of the local chapter lived in Peabody and had two Dobermans. I was out riding around, looking for loose dogs when the dispatcher sent me to an address with a complaint about two Dobermans running loose causing trouble. No problem. I went to the address and knocked on the door. A big guy opens the door and just looks at me. I introduced myself, "Hi, I'm Nancy the Dog Officer and I had a complaint about your two Dobermans". He just looked at me. Seemed like a few minutes, probably wasn't and he says to me "I like your badge, what would you do if I took your badge?" I looked back at him and told him he wasn't big enough to take my badge. He had no clue who he was dealing with and neither did I have any clue who I was dealing with. He started to laugh and told me he liked me. He invited me in for coffee. I still have no clue who he is. I walked into a house full of antiques, nice antiques and told him how much I liked his collection. I told him I had complaints about his dogs, asked him if he was letting them run loose and he admitted he was. I told him he needed to keep them on his own property for a number of reasons but mostly because he lived on a main drag and they could get hit by a car, and if that happened, he was not going to like the person I became. He asked me if I thought I was tough. I just replied "Yeah". He had a little chuckle. He then asked me if he called me regarding his neighbor's dogs bothering his dogs if I would take care of that too. I said "Why wouldn't I?" He then informed me of his status in the Hell's Angels. I told him I could care less who he was, my main concern was the dogs. A few days later he called to tell me his neighbors dogs were in his yard bothering his dogs. I told him I would handle it and went and spoke to his neighbor. Seems the gentleman was a guy with a Napoleon complex, big mouth, short stature, know it all. I advised him he may not like a woman telling him what to do, but if he wanted trouble, the Hell's Angel living down the street, whose dogs his dogs were bothering might not take too kindly to him. That shut the little guy up quick. Homer, the Hell's Angel was now my friend and if I ever needed anything, to let him know. Nice to have some leverage in my back pocket. Meanwhile, back at the station, the guys kept asking how everything went at the call with the Dobermans. I just said the guy was a gentleman and I wouldn't get anymore calls about his dogs. Revenge backfired on them. I never let patrolmen know that I knew who Homer was.

The Owl

The High School called me one day and told me that one of the maintenance men noticed an owl lying on the ground behind the building. It wasn't moving and he didn't want to touch it. I took a ride up expecting to see a dead owl laying there but that wasn't the case. The owl was alive, his eyes were closed and I can only imagine the headache he must have had. The back of the school is north facing and the building has the darkened glass windows, not your average sized windows, these are the big windows used mostly in cafeterias, which is what was behind the glass. He was laying right beside the building, odd place to find an owl I thought, I grabbed a towel out of my van and wrapped him up in it, just his head was peeking out. I decided not to put him in a crate and instead just held him while I drove back to the station. He definitely is not feeling well. I called the local vet I used, who also was the vet for one of the zoos in the area and described what I was seeing. He advised taking the owl into the raptor expert at Tufts. Tufts is an hour or more, depending on traffic away. I think I'll ask for a ride. I went to the Chief, showed him the owl and asked if he could spare someone to drive us to Tufts mainly because I was concerned that putting him in a crate could cause more harm to him. The Chief was an animal lover, I got my ride. A patrolman named Bob offered to drive us in. We were going along on our journey and were probably about 25 minutes away when I looked down and saw the lice moving around on his head. Now I know lice won't jump species, in other words, bird lice will not infect a person, they just give you the creeps. Well it seems at the same time I saw the lice, so did Bob. He screams "What is that on his head?" I turned my head and kind of whispered "lice". He screams "What?" I looked at him and told him lice. He uses a little profanity then tells me "I want a head count before you get out of this vehicle!" I ignored him. We arrived at Tufts, specifically the bird center and was met by a very nice veterinarian, a one limb amputee who used crutches and we were escorted into his exam room. He had the coolest job. Outside was a huge fenced in aviary with a bald eagle in it. Seems he was recuperating from a wing injury and was out there to get his wing strength back. Inside were all these boxes lined up, similar to giant bird houses with tilted roofs and locked latches. This is where the owls are kept, in the dark the way they like it, until it's their turn to use the aviary.

He examined my owl and told me he thought he had a concussion and that he would take him in and treat him. He also showed us, by peeling back some feathers on the owl's head, his inner ear. He told us that owl's have a symbiotic relationship with a bug that lives in the inner ear, but our owl didn't have one. He told me he would call me when the owl was ready to come home so he could be released where he was found.

I went back to the school to look the area over to try and figure out what had caused the concussion. I don't know if it was human or just accidental, but best to see the area in the dark, which is when he would have been most active. I went around the back of the school to where I picked him up. There was a full moon, just like the night before and look at that, the moon is reflecting off the glass and a picture appeared in my brain. I pictured a rodent running alongside the building and the owl coming in for a quick grab thinking he could just fly up towards the moon but he crashed into the glass, lucky for the rodent if my observation and assumption is right.

About two weeks later I got the call that the owl had made a full recovery and I could come and get him. I drove out and met up with the vet to get the whole run down on the owls' health. Tufts had banded him, in case of any future problems and for tracking purposes and he was doing really well. I drove back to the school to find a small posse of bird watchers and the local photographer waiting. People like to listen to police scanners, that's the only way they would have known about this. No problem, as long as they listen and give the owl room I don't see any harm, I would be interested too. When I was carrying him around hurt he never moved, just kept his head still and his eyes closed, which is how I remembered him so it came as a little shock, even knowing they can spin their heads around, when I took him out to place him on the boulder I picked out for release and he spun his head around and looked at me. It was kind of funny. The owl looked around, listened to the sounds of the sparrows going crazy because he was back and then took off up into the trees. Happy ending for the owl, a beautiful Barred Owl.

Rat Dawg

I received a call one day from a gentleman I will call Mr. H, in a neighboring town that had no Dog Officer. He started telling me about a dog he had named Lady that was very afraid of people and had recently had a litter of four puppies. This man was feeding her and trying to get her to trust him but nothing was working for him and he turned to me for help. I took a ride over to the neighborhood he lived in, on my own time, and sat and watched for a while to see what was going on. Lady was a mixed Shephard/Doberman mutt, not a big dog, not overly skinny and obviously getting fed well by Mr. H. I knocked on his door and asked him to show me where the puppies were so I could check on them and see how old they were. I was also hoping that Lady would try to protect them from me and I could possibly grab her. The puppies were about six weeks old, eyes were open and they were cute, fat, fuzzy balls of fur. Lady kept her distance, all the while barking at me, but never approaching, afraid to even protect her puppies. Most mothers will fiercely protect their pups, but she was just too scared of people. I took the puppies with me and would come back to focus on getting her. Of course puppies are always the first to be adopted out, so after they spent a few weeks at the vets getting shots and handled and checked out, they were adopted out. Now I need to catch Lady. My first attempt was using a large Havahart trap, loaded up with food. I caught every animal in the neighborhood, skunk, raccoon, house cat, a loose dog, but no Lady. Ok, I don't like using the tranquilizer gun but I think it's my only chance. I don't like shooting animals, so I enlisted one of the guys from the station to help me. What a sight we must have been. Brownie was a big burly guy, (big animal lover) with a shot gun style tranquilizer gun running through backyards with a young lady chasing after a dog. We had notified the police station in the town we were in that we would be doing this just in case the calls came in, and they did. Brownie shot her in the rump with the tranquilizer dart, but she ran and hid and we couldn't find her, so much for that tactic. We went hunting several more times, but she was onto us, we never saw her again. It was getting cold, it was now the middle of December and I hadn't heard from Mr. H. It was my birthday and I was laying on the couch watching TV when the phone rang. A young girl called to tell me that she had a dog follow her dog into the house and it seemed scared, she lived in Mr. H's neighborhood. I went to her address and sure enough, it was Lady. I took her to the vet or dog pound as it now was and booked her in. I decided to have her spayed and try to find her a home. After her 10 day stint and her spaying, she came to my house. I had a room that I kept my horse blankets in, sort of a mud room I guess you would call it and she went right over and laid down on the horse blankets. She seemed very comfortable there, until you approached her. She would sit up and stare into your eyes, never losing eye contact, she was worried about me and what I would do to her. I gently took her paw in my hand, stroked the top of it and while looking back into her eyes, told her I would never hurt her. She took her paw slowly back, continuing to keep eye contact and laid back down. For the next two weeks we went through this routine while I looked to find her a home of her own. She would go with me during the day in the truck and I was trying to build back her trust in mankind, something she surely did not have. On one particular day I gave a ride to a friend who smoked. Lady was sitting between us in my truck and when he lit up a cigarette she panicked, jumped into my lap and was shaking terribly. I yelled for him to throw the cigarette out and pulled the truck over to calm her down. That one moment told me a lot. If you listen to animals, they will tell you their stories and this one was not a good one.

I found an older woman looking for a dog who had no kids in the house, I didn't know if kids would throw her over the deep end and thought an older person, low key, would suit her better. She also was a non-smoker. I dropped Lady off, but not for long. She called three hours later telling me that Lady was trying to get out the windows of her house. I went back and picked her up. We spent another three weeks, same routine with the paw while I searched for another home. This time I found a gentleman in a wheelchair looking for a companion to keep him company. She went to his house but lasted only two days. The man was heartbroken because she wouldn't come anywhere near him, she didn't even want him to put the clip on her for her to go out on a run he had set up for her. When he did get her on the run, she went to the end of it and refused to come in, he had to keep calling his daughter to come and help him with Lady. Lady came back to my house again. The gentleman's daughter dropped her off and I put her in the house while I spoke with her and got the story of what she was doing. I went back in the house and she was lying on her horse blankets. I sat down and looked at her and said to her "What am I going to do with you?" She raised her leg and gave me her paw. "Oh, you want to stay with me?" OK. She now became my best friend, we went everywhere together. I took her to the barn with me and decided to see if she would stick around, off leash, while I rode my horse. It had rained hard earlier in the day and there were a lot of big puddles in the paddock. I was riding, all the time trying to keep an eye on her to make sure she didn't take off and saw her lay in one of the deep puddles and crawl through it on her stomach. She came out soaked. I looked at her and said "Look at you, you look like a drowned rat, what are you, a rat dog?" She wagged her tail. I asked her "You like that name, rat dog?" She wagged her tail again. This was the first time I had seen her wag her tail since she had been with me. Ok, I guess your name is Rat Dawg, I had to spell it a little different and an old cartoon came to mind, Deputy Dawg.

Rat Dawg and I were inseparable. It still took a little over a year for her to venture out of the room where the horse blankets were. It was just her safe spot, but she did eventually trust me and my husband enough to join us in other rooms. One night she got up and was walking cockeyed, not normal, looks neurologic, I panicked, called the vet and the only thing that I could get out was her name. I broke down crying. He told me to bring her right over. Seems he was getting ready to go out to a hockey game in Boston, but would wait to see us. He looked at her and told me she either had a brain tumor or old dog disease. If it was old dog disease, she would be fine in about three days, if not, then it was probably a brain tumor. It wasn't old dog disease. She couldn't get up, she couldn't even lift her head, she just laid still. I loaded her into my truck and took her to the vet. The vet offered to carry her in and I said "No, she is my dog, I will carry her and I will be with her until it's over." He understood. I put her up on the exam table, she started shaking, she was scared, she knew, they all know and that's the heartbreaking part. I firmly believe you should never let a friend die alone or with strangers. If you love them then let them go. I held her and patted her and told her she would always be with me because she had become a very big part of my heart. She passed peacefully in my arms as I cried like a baby. Her ashes are still in a special place in my house and always will be and I know she will be waiting for me when I cross that bridge.

In writing my stories I'm hoping that this will encourage more women to get into the field of Animal Law Enforcement. In 95% of most households it is the woman who feeds the dogs, cats, etc which always made my job easier. They hear a woman's voice, hear the word "cookie" and they come running. You don't have the packs of dogs roaming around as I did back in the 70s and 80s, but saving animals and prosecuting those deserving of it, is very rewarding. There is also the heartbreak but I would always think to myself, get mad, get even for the animal, you can mourn later in your own way but get justice first.

Dedicated to Judge Tiffany, Rat Dawg and all the patrolmen I enjoyed torturing for 16 years.

About the Author

I'm a firm believer that your age or gender does not define you, it is what is in your heart and how you apply yourself to the task that you choose, in my case, animals were always first and foremost in my life and they still are. I enjoy learning about all animals and having the opportunity to work with so many different animals was the best time of my life, I hope you enjoy reading about it.